ב"ה

לה"י

This Book Belongs To:

Please Read It To Me!

Dovid
The Little Shepherd

By Dina Rosenfeld

Drawings by Ilene Winn-Lederer

Hachai
PUBLISHING

בס"ד

Also in this series:
A Little Boy Named Avram
Kind Little Rivka
A Little Girl Named Miriam

Dovid the Little Shepherd

For my uncle, and all the little Dovids who bear his name. D.R.

With love to, Jeffrey, Joshua, Ira, Malkeleah and David E.
who share my dreams- past, present and future. I.W.L.

First Edition Adar 5756 / March 1996
Second Impression Cheshvan 5763 / November 2002
Third Impression Nissan 5765 / April 2005
Forth Impression Shevat 5770 / January 2010

ISBN-13: 978-0-922613-67-0
ISBN-10: 0-922613-67-2
LCCN: 94-77373

Hachai Publishing
Brooklyn, NY
Tel: (718) 633-0100 Fax: (718) 633-0103
www.hachai.com - info@hachai.com

Manufactured in Hong Kong, January 2010 by Paramount Printing

Once upon a time in the Land of Israel, there lived a little boy named Dovid.

Dovid's father had many sheep.
Most of the sheep were white, and some of them were black. They had bright shiny eyes, wet black noses, and thick curly coats.

There were big strong sheep who liked to run quickly and butt their heads together.

There were old tired sheep who walked slowly and carefully over the mountains.

And there were frisky baby lambs who climbed on the rocks and played "follow the leader."

Sheep need someone to watch them and take care of them. A person who does this job is called a shepherd.

Even though Dovid was just a little boy, he was a very good shepherd for his father's sheep. If a sheep wandered into the woods, Dovid hurried to bring it back to the flock.

If lions or bears growled on the hills at night, Dovid lit fires to keep them away.

If a baby sheep fell down and got hurt, Dovid would hold the frightened lamb in his arms, stroking it gently to make it feel better.

One day, the little shepherd led his flock to a beautiful meadow for a meal of juicy green grass.

The big sheep ate and ate until they were full. But the old sheep and the little lambs just walked away, their black noses drooping down to the ground.

"Something is wrong," thought Dovid.

"Maybe they don't like this grass."

So Dovid led the flock to another green field.

He watched as the old sheep and the little lambs ran happily toward the meadow. But the big strong sheep ran faster on their big strong legs.

They bit off big mouthfuls of soft green grass and ate it all up!

"Baa baa," sighed the old sheep,
"Baa baa," cried the little lambs,

By the time they came to the meadow,
there was no soft grass left for them!

Dovid was worried.

"If the old sheep don't eat," he thought,
"they will be too weak to walk over the
mountains. If the baby lambs don't eat,
how will they grow up to be big and strong?"

Dovid had no one to ask for advice. He had to think of a way to help the hungry sheep all by himself. He thought and thought.

At last he had a plan.

The sheep watched curiously as Dovid set to work. He chopped down some trees, split them into rails, and built three round fences.

The little shepherd led all the big strong sheep behind the first fence.

"What a nice fence," thought the big sheep. They began to sharpen their horns against the wood.

Then Dovid led all the old weak sheep behind the second fence.

"What a nice fence," thought the old sheep. They began to scratch their backs against the rails.

Finally, Dovid led all the little lambs behind the third fence.

"What a nice fence," thought the baby lambs. They poked their little heads through the holes to see what would happen next.

At feeding time, Dovid let the baby lambs come out first. They nibbled and nibbled the soft sweet top part of the grass with their small baby teeth.

Next, Dovid let the old sheep have their turn. They munched and munched the juicy middle part of the grass with their old weak teeth.

Finally, Dovid let the big sheep come out. They gobbled and gobbled the crunchy bottom part of the grass with their big strong teeth.

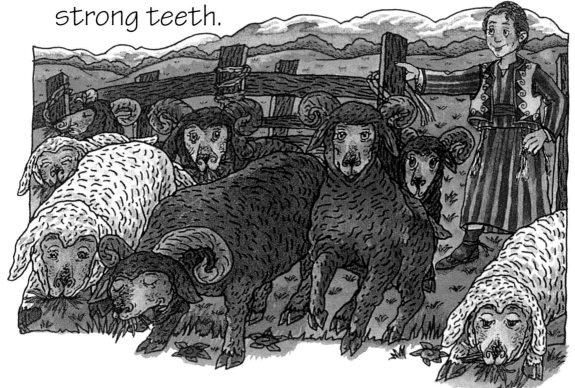

Now, all the sheep were happy.
They lay down side by side to dream of the green meadows where Dovid would take them tomorrow.

The little shepherd was happy. He sat down under the trees with his harp to sing songs to Hashem, the Creator of the World.

Hashem was happy, too.

He said, "Just as Dovid has taken care of every single sheep, I know he will take good care of every single Jew – young and old, big and small. Let him be their king!"

And so it was that Dovid, the little shepherd, grew up to become Dovid HaMelech, King of Israel.

<u>A NOTE TO PARENTS AND TEACHERS:</u>

Dovid HaMelech (King David) was born in the year 2854 (907 B.C.E.) in Israel. Like many other great Jewish leaders, Dovid spent his early years as a shepherd. While tending the sheep, young Dovid displayed boundless care and concern for them. This essential trait is one of the characteristics that qualified him for the exalted position of king.

In Jewish thought, a king serves as a model for the Jewish nation's relationship with G-d, the King of kings. A human king's devotion to Torah study and the performance of mitzvot inspires his subjects to do the same. The people's self-nullification to their king teaches them to nullify themselves before G-d.

Therefore, unlike the kings of other nations, a Jewish monarch is not chosen for his physical strength and stature. Dovid was chosen to rule because of his devotion to G-d and the Jewish people, for his piety, Torah scholarship and refined spiritual qualities.

At the tender age of thirty, Dovid began to rule over the tribe of Judah. After seven years, the elders of all the tribes requested that Dovid be their king as well. In 2892 (869 B.C.E.), Dovid became king of the entire Jewish nation and made Jerusalem his capital.

G-d promised Dovid that the royal dynasty would remain within his family forever. The future Jewish king, Moshiach, will come from the House of Dovid. Moshiach will re-establish the monarchy, rebuild the Holy Temple and reunite all of the Jewish people. This will mark the beginning of the Messianic Era, a time when the world will become a place of peace, prosperity, wisdom and harmony.

We hope your child will be inspired to take care of others with love and sensitivity just like little Dovid.

D. Rosenfeld

This story is based on the
Midrash: (Shmos Rabba 2:2)